RECLINE FAR DOWN

JILLIAN ADAMS

ISBN: 978-1-4907-3963-2 (sc)
ISBN: 978-1-4907-3962-5 (e)

Trafford rev. 06/19/2014

www.trafford.com

North America & international
toll-free: 1 888 232 4444 (USA & Canada)
fax: 812 355 4082

1:30 A.M.

I still have the nightmare
Of waking up to you and your
Dry, cold face, just as
That man in the paper did.

Your death gray eyes looking
At my pale blue ones,
As if to say "I'm here,
Do you recognize me?"

My eyes are painfully focused
On your decrepit face,
Whilst yours are wondering away
To a shadow on the wall.

In five minutes, either one of
Our lives could end
In this moment and you would
Still feel nothing.

Your family's forced love can't
Protect you from cruel reality
I blink to take in the images, crossed with thoughts ... and I wake.

STRINGS ON THEIR FINGERS

I put a string around my finger yesterday,

For no particular reason, not to remember anything,

Not to remind myself of something I will

Inevitably end up forgetting

Despite the common man's foolish efforts

To make fads and look normal to others;

No, just because I had loose string on me.

I don't believe in myself.

I believe in other people to make me believe

A religion, a deity, a loaf of bread.

It is their calling. No wait. It is

Their DUTY to make me believe something that they

Have to. "Duty" is a funny word.

I love my friends.

They, unfortunately, are all common.

The common man is not a fool,

Not as foolish as someone who is normal,

Not nearly as foolish as having strings give a purpose to you.

My friends all have strings on their fingers.

WIND (PROPERLY PUBLISHED)

Wind

Whistling, Rustling

Moving, Whirling, Swirling

Running around the world

Nature!

GLOOM OF WINTER

It was bitterly cold and snowy,

The trees were bare and skinny,

There was no one outside,

Everyone was safely inside,

There, where dogs desperately wanted to go out.

But a bad and windy blizzard had formed,

Suddenly the power was dead,

There was no good hope.

THE MIGHTY FLUFF

Fluff
Fluff for window treatment stuff
On the tops of our heads
On men so gruff

Gray
Gray in the bay
The sky was once blue
That's why no one wanted to stay

Light
Light is your touch
Gentle is your fingers
We don't say too much

Low
Low is your toe
Gently poking my ankle
To you, I'll never say "no"

Pretty
Pretty is your face, your race

With you I'm at a loss for words
With you my heart's in the write place

Hopeful
Hopeful and not mope-full
I hope you will accept me
I hope you will never be nope-full

Love
Love is all I feel for you
It is love that were making
It is our virginity were taking

Of this, and of you, I will never get enough,
So here is to you; The Mighty Fluff.

TODAY

Pretty drunk people
Licking up their own vomit
Forcing themselves to smile
For the World Wide Web

PAINTINGS OF LEX

I'll take you away
To the inner mechanisms
Of your mind, whether you like it
Or not.

My feelings are definitely
Unhappy ones, so they are
Obviously nostalgic ones.
You should know this by now.

You made me this way.
You don't even know this, but
It's all of your fault.
All of it is yours.

Now you can blame the Bible,
You can blame your family,
You can blame Harry Styles,
And you can blame yourself.

Do not blame me,
For it is not my fault.

I had some things to do with
Your life; but not that much.

Your wretched lies,
Your blue eyes,
Your gentle face,
Your black lace.

Do not come to my house.
I do not like you,
I am obsessed with you.
But you have done evil sins.

Go to your ugly society,
Drink your red wine,
Try to make yourself decent
For the world, And for
The people that love you...

That's me.

So Yeah...

Laughing in the bar
Drinking in the car
Letting bygones be bygones
We don't drive far

Field mice run across roads
We squash rats, squirrels, and toads
We are deep, far in the wheat grains
Our drunk imagination unloads

I WONDER, I BLOODY WONDER

I went to church today,

I sat in the back.

I saw many butts.

"An ass attack".

This may sound rude,

This may sound crass,

You may stop reading now;

But listen to the poem, it's not just about the ass...

Each seat had an imprint.

Each one showed a single mark of life.

Then I suddenly thought, a horrific thought;

What if each one were to take themselves out with a knife?

Not just a knife, maybe a gun,

Or a pipe, or some pencils, or a pair of scissors,

Belts, bags, or leap out of the window in self-shun?

Depression! Oh, sweet depression!

Why must you perform your horror show?

Why must you make us hate everything,

And fill us with such woe?

Then I began to wonder...

I wonder, I bloody wonder...
How many of these people are really pure?
How many wouldn't steal?
Or slam theirs, or someone else's, face in the door?

I wonder, I bloody wonder...
How many women have been raped?
How long must there be discrimination
On sex, ethnicity, religion, or shape?

I wonder, I bloody wonder...
Why must important things be so long?
Scriptures, school, work, contracts, and conferences,
Surely something must be wrong.

I wonder, I bloody wonder
What's up with the wars?
All those fine, once humane people dying
All those poor, poor families crying.
Is this the way for America to stay safe,
By lying?

I wonder, I bloody wonder...
Why must all good things come to an end?
The sunsets, the world one day perhaps,

Or staying with a close friend?

I wonder, I bloody wonder...
Why must people abuse animals?
Do it on something that deserves it more,
Like pedophiles, terrorists, or cannibals.

I wonder, I bloody wonder...
What is the meaning of life?
Are we all really here or... wait a minute!
Wasn't I first talking about people taking themselves with a knife?

How did I get here anyhow?!
Hmmm...

I wonder, I bloody wonder...

Bi-Sanity

I like my craziness,
And it likes me.
I look after my craziness,
As it looks after me.

But I am not just crazy,
I can be sane.
It all depends on how I am feeling.
There are other lives inside my brain.

Some days I may kill you.
Some days I may save you.
Some days I may hate you.
Some days I may love you.

MUSH

Mushy mush

Wet taboo

Inside my head

Which one are you?

GINA MAE

Gina Mae,

She began to pray,

That she would get a puppy for Christmas.

Gina Mae,

She began to pray,

That Donny Osmond would be her first kiss.

Gina Mae,

She began to pray,

That she could go on a date with Max McWard.

Gina Mae,

She began to pray,

That she would finally get that new Blue Ford.

Gina Mae,

She began to pray,

That she would get the engagement ring from her dream.

Gina Mae,

She began to pray,

That her new boss won't be as mean.

Gina Mae,

She began to pray,

That this will be a better marriage.

Gina Mae,

She began to pray,

That she can buy the expensive baby carriage.

Gina Mae,

She began to pray,

That she could beat the 5k run.

Gina Mae,

She began to pray,

That she could get her hands undone.

DEAR FRIEND

Dear Friend

Do not go to war

You'll just be another disappointed soul

Running, Screaming, ducking

Drinking heavily when you come home

I don't give a damn about Uncle Sam

But I give a hoot about you

BRONZE SLUMBERZ

Wish there was a way
For me to leave home.
I know one day,
I'll leave home.

I need sleep first,
I need to rest my eyes.
Please someone sing me
A lullaby.

I want to leave here
So I can be an artist.
It's 11:00,
Street lights.

I'm up.
Should I walk?
No.
Just lay here with my Bronze Slumberz talk.

DONOVAN THE SKELETON AND LARRY THE TURTLE (PART 1)

Now I don't know if you have heard but
Donovan the Skeleton is the word
His mind is on his love
Named Larry the Turtle who is in
Puerto Rico smoking grass
With his best friends and drinking Beaujolais
No recognition of his last girlfriend's ass

Donovan the Skeleton will beat the shit out of
Larry the Turtle; publicly and when he least expects it
It will not be on the news
When Donovan and his crews
Of rough zombies rise from the pews
To sleep with his prostitute Roxy the Bug
And give them each a lick on the face and a hug

A

A quaff of mangy hair
Sits on a damp window sill.
The wind gently plays with it
Whilst blowing the grains of wheat.

A cool mist than rises up
From the depths of ground
And kisses slowly, sweetly,
The dew-soaked grass.

A pair of child's rain boots
Sits near the muddy doorstep,
Wondering and waiting, if
They will be loved again.

A man smokes a pipe
While his Border Collie runs about.
He looks up at a cloudy
Sun and, whimsically, smiles.

YOU HYPOCRITICAL TURD

The longest time of their lives,
They have been raised this way.
For more or less,
It is the best,
So it would be better if they stay.

I never drove you off.
I never made you go.
Taking up the wide stairs,
Not possible; but who cares,
You still don't know what I know.

The concept of law
Has no heaven or hell.
That's what you teach,
That's what you preach,
But you're still spoiled rotten.

DONOVAN THE SKELETON AND LARRY THE TURTLE (PART 2)

Donovan and Larry

Aren't a very scary

Couple to smoke weed with

Unless you make their list

Of people they should take a piss

On after they miss their

Their curfew.

"Do you remember rock and roll radio?"

Asked Larry to the potato.

He didn't know

And anyways, he had to go.

There was a protest down the road

Being held by Allen the Toad

A protest, a very large one at that,

About the unfair death of Myrna the Wombat.

Myrna the Wombat

Was killed by a white cat

For trespassing on

The house of the Gibbon

There's nothing unfair about that

The unfairness was in fact

That Bonzo the Rat

Could come and enjoy the gibbon prostitutes as he please

But Myrna's father Bruce

Who wasn't too loose

Could only have fun if he brought the landlord to his knees.

So Bruce

The now violent and loose

Took matters into his paws

And foolishly took it to the law

So no one, not even he

Could have a good time in a tree

With a gibbon named Kissy Vamoose

Bonzo the Rat

Had owned several a cat

Who could do a dirty job

On this wombat slob

For depriving him of his good fun

So Bruce's daughter was found there

On Anastasia the Shoe's front stairs

All bloody and beaten

So Allen the Toad

Marched down the western road
Saying, "This bastard rat should be eaten!"

Stray cats
And rebel rats
Drunken sloths
Hobo moths
And mutated place mats.

All of these unusual anarchists
In the big wide road
Were helping Donovan, Larry, Roxy
Support Allen the Toad
The rebel cats hadn't eaten in a while
And the thought of munching on Bonzo made them smile

Donovan the Skeleton and Larry the Turtle
Were stoned out of their minds
And wearing gibbon girdles
To be in support of poor Myrna and her sniffling father
So they burned Bonzo the Rat's house down that day
While pumping fists and screaming out "Minority" by Green Day
It is definitely a possible task for all immortals
To be like Donovan the Skeleton and Larry the Turtle...

UNJUST

The criminal paced his way,

He did not rush at all,

To the car he went and there he stayed.

He hid under the seat until the cops passed.

He was successful in this,

For he was the last

Criminal to get away.

Although, 2 out of 3 criminals were

Actually innocent anyways.

He had a R.A.P. sheet as long as he was

For things such as

Assault and high jacking a bus

But that didn't seem to matter

To all of the "heroes" in court,

The ones who shoot defenseless motorists

And announce false reports.

The ones who kill teens in their custody,

"They crashed their heads in the back seat." they say

But doesn't anybody notice,

That it's different than the story they told yesterday?

Anyhow, there was no evidence to support

That the white criminal did the crime,

But they said the two black ones,

Should definitely do time.

Even though they had no weapon to show,

The black men claimed that the white one wielded a gun.

But in court that's not how things go.

The two black men were found falsely guilty

As the white man smiled,

There was just no chance

In this unfair, retarded trial.

So with that,

The white criminal met people,

And was on the cover of Rolling Stone and TIME,

And helped Billy Graham preach on his steeple.

He could spread out his legs

And relax on the sand,

Despite the fact he secretly knew

He just killed a man.

BITCH

Your name is not even enough

And besides, it degrades my dog.

How dare you take away the man I so dearly love?!

If you loved him, why did you leave him heartbroken, you old hog?

I hope you die alone

More than my wish that you never existed.

Your poem deserve only two stanzas

Since your neediness and false love persisted.

For Nelson Mandela

I will spread your beauty

Throughout the valleys

Of the human race

They will hopefully understand

My mind is unhealthy

The time I spend writing this

Is time I could be dying

I hope somehow you of all people

Would understand

BYE-BYE (SEE YOU SOON)

Don't worry about me
For now, I'm fine
I don't need relationships
Nobody needs to be mine

I'm functional (somewhat) now
I have confidence now because of you
It was a pleasure having you around
I hope you feel the same way too

Although, you deserve someone better
Yeah, someone a lot, tougher
Smarter, cooler, more social;
But it's been a ball being your lover

LONG-HAIRED BOYS

Almost all my life,
I've been fascinated with long hair.
It doesn't matter if it's product filled,
It doesn't matter if it goes "there";
If it's constantly growing,
It can go anywhere

My hair is short,
We share a love/hate relationship.
I wish it could grow long.
Sometimes I think short hair is shit,
Then I know it is easier to wash.
Boys, honestly, might look better with it.

In the days of Columbus, Shakespeare,
Maybe even Jesus Himself,
Having long hair was a good thing,
A sign of good wealth;
But now it's a label.
For example: Emo, Goth, no good health.

Rock stars sport it,

Some bikers may,

Skaters definitely might,

There are still mullets at bay.

Yet, there could still be a risk

Of driving people away.

Adults mostly,

Maybe a few douchy kids;

But they will grab attention.

Everyone thinks they know exactly everything the boy did.

At first glance, they assume

That he would sell or buy pot for a couple quid.

Even if we look biker-ish, people judge.

Once, an old woman was in line,

Kroger, a bandanna was around my head.

She could have <u>pretended</u> it was all fine,

Instead the old bitch called me out.

I will never forget that shitty swine.

Just for the record, drugs ain't me.

No interest in them, nor any violence,

But who cares if I did?

It is just plain common sense.

I probably won't assault you.
<u>You</u> can do bad things past tense.

You might do it again,
Or you may not, but the ones
Who do it again are put away.
So when you see long haired biker-ish boys,
You probably won't be in any danger,
<u>MAYBE</u> you will live to see another day.

FOLK SONG (A HAIKU FOR ANYONE WHO WANTS TO LISTEN)

Little rebel boy,

Will sing "We shall overcome".

Many sang with him.

VIRGIN SNOW

You are unthreaded as well as
Well spoken for.
Beautiful droplets of your children
Land in the white womb
Of your full body.

You don't fret over
The small stuff,
Such as births and deaths.
You weep, however,
Over the importance of spaghetti sauce.

But you are just a white,
Unkempt mound of snow on a large
And vast sloping hill...
What would you know about such motherly things?
Yet, this does not mean you lack superior intelligence or beauty.

ELOQUENCE NOWHERE

Time goes by through the rings of my mind
Like a wind through a wild plain
Where buffalos and other hooved animals graze.
Time will tell when flowers grow,
When leaves turn gray and brown,
When snow will fall,
And when life will begin itself again and again.

The time of a minute is not measured
Enough for its great strength and velocity.
You can kill or be friends with a man in a minute.
It can be good or bad, fun and exciting,
Or devastatingly boring; painfully embarrassing.

Do not take your time on anything
For granted.
It may be a precious moment between
Your, or your loved one's life and death

Time is important to the meager lives of which we lead
Of which our family leads,
Of our good friends,
Of all of your loved ones,
And of yourself.

RED WATERWORKS

Red waterworks
Flowing freely through the wet
Scummy dry eyelids of mine
Wet onto my finger tips
Wet on the walls
Of my painful dead brain

Dead, dead is my soul
Wait for my love to prosper
Wet is my eyes
Cool is the air in the room
Red is my blood
White is the ends of my nostrils

Cool, cool breeze is wetting my
Eyes even more, it hurts
Not nearly as much as
My heart hurts after you broke it
It had been broken for a long while
Not that you care

Your mascara runs down your face
And imprints into your hands

It is black like your icy heart
While I have a cold drink
You lap up the blood
You spilled last night

Your pair of friends arrive at the house
You laugh as you speak to them gently
You speak to me horridly
It is all my fault, I know
But must you bring it up every time we speak?
I still love you, you know

FICTIONAL TOWN

Morribone Telsa
Is a fictional town.
The ladder of fictional literature
Has been cut in an unknown
Place to their insane rounds
Where intoxicants go down.

Wet hands may sculpt the sculpture,
But the sticky fingers turn it.
The material used to build the sculpture
Is what will really hold it together.
Your soul may burn it,
And then you will not ever earn it.

WEST WINDS FROM THE "PASSED ON"

Oh which winds can bring themselves

Down to their knees in unknowing

Self-worship?

You know which ones you are

If you can tell the super powers

Of God the Almighty Leader

As well as feel the unity of the spirit of oneness.

To you, I will salute,

Since you can only feel

How you impact me as a person;

And although I'm just another mortal soul on this earth,

I hope that I will not come across as a petty necrophiliac, but a fan.

I love you, to all who influence me,

Especially you, John W.O. Lennon, rest in peace.

A Shirt to Mark 33 Years

I forgot to wear a shirt that would mark 33 years.

J. Lennon was killed 33 years ago yesterday,

But no one really cared.

It makes me sad that our generation is that lost

And there really isn't that much hope for the future

peacemakers.

So today I wore, accidentally, Pink Floyd.

Not many people cared much either,

But it got doors open for me,

So I was momentarily happy.

I will wear my Beatles shirt tomorrow.

TREES OF YESTERDAY

Sun risin' over the trees,

The yesterdays do not judge.

They felt the love of the sun too.

As has everyone else.

I watch the sun say "Bye".

I keep walking, unnoticed,

Then I unintentionally leave it forever

In my memory box.

SOME FATEFUL NIGHT

Under a pale blue moon,
You take your time with the
Pretty faces on your colorful pictures.
Except you don't know what your
Man will do next while you
Trace out his broken features.

Take your own life and break all
Rules, the people will judge,
The leaders are fools.
Except you can't tell any difference
Between reality and his mind.

His mind, unknown to all, other
Than a divine spirit,
Tells your art how to behave.
You don't mind the imperfections
Whilst this man lusts for all of
The beauty you once gave.

The past replays the present
And interrupts your rebellion.
You give no recognition to

His personality which resembles a
Old trampled medallion.

A beautiful rose sits on the
Table and you manage to capture
It's mystics in your simple drawing
As you let out a sigh, and try
To get as much done, neatly,
Before morning's surprise dawning.

You realize your subject's strength
Breaks, as if it were a soft
Layer of ground in monstrous earthquakes.
You still don't notice if
He can sense apprehension.

As you see tears drizzle
Down his face, it hits you
That there is no going
Back to what was,
Or what is...
Anyways it messes up your drawing.

As You Wake Up

Babies, dogs, and soldiers crawl
On their bellies for
Transportation, Entertainment,
Or to get what they want.

Some people get what they want
By means of intoxication,
Of greed and eating much,
Of love and of theft.

Like the evil rich brat who slain four people
Says "Being spoiled is a mental illness!"
And the court believed it.
So now he's riding horses in California for 10 years

But there's more...

A mindless freak of nature
Kills his whole family
Including his deformed brother
And is labeled dangerous.

An artist gets a paper cut
On his canvas and bleeds
To death while screaming psalms.
Front page news in National Enquirer.

A woman missed her husband in
Iraq, so she fed their newborn
Child to him when he came home.
He said it was delicious.

These and many more exciting
Stories can be yours!
Just lift your head up and
Press the button labeled snooze!

VIRGIN

If you want to do it then we can.
All I want is your soft hand,
Upon my largest organ.
Enter my gates, created by man.

Dead skin breaks off,
Princesses become call girls,
Just as Princes become frogs,
All are losing touch of morals.

My friends find humor
In the ugly side of pleasure,
Though it could be beauty,
With love going unmeasured.

Please take me in your kingdom,
I know I'm just an ugly farm girl.
But I just want to build a bridge
Connecting passion with my world.

VIRILITY

For your man
You will feed him meat.
May you and he never
Be rich or poor.
But especially him.

The man is a figure of wisdom,
A figure of experience.
He doesn't not care
About women or children,
Hardly about his fellow man,
Definitely about himself.

May HIS life be wealthy,
May HIS weights be heavy,
To the point where elephants
Look like Edward Cullen
Trying to lift them up.

May you pray to be a man.
You will never be as worthy
As he with the penis.
So make yourself useful
And make Himself dinner.
Sincerely Yours, Majority of Society

MORE THAN (PART 1)

More than a pimp-
A misplaced lover.
A mistreated son...
An unhappy marriage.

Cold eyes,
Practically homeless,
Moving from frat home to frat home,
Looking for real work.

The female prostitute
Might take notice,
Might be a victim,
But we're not too sure.

He wants love,
But needs lots of help.
At least he's not as misplaced,
As the un-faithful man.

MORE THAN (PART 2)

More than a school shooter,

A hated young boy,

Hating himself

Was in a competition with others

An unhappy student who needed psychiatry

Got crucified with lies instead.

He had to die

Along with everyone else.

This is not an excuse

For beyond evil actions,

More like an attempt for an understanding...

If there is any.

A foolish boy once told me,

"Bullying isn't a big deal."

We'll see if he changes his opinion

When a bullet encounters his forehead.

PISSED IN SALT LAKE CITY AGAIN: PART IV (A HAIKU)

In the ugly bar,

I wish I was with RuPaul,

But not in this time.

WHALE MY WHALE

Whale my whale,
How do I tell,
How sweet is your flat breasts?
More sweet than the rest.

Whale my whale
Your mind is not well
Whenever you try to eat,
Your own flattened feet.

Whale my whale
Your body is for sale
That is not how it should be,
Trust me, you can take it from me.

Whale my whale
Do not eat kale.
You are a sea creature
Your blowhole is your greatest feature.

Whale my whale
Please whale, tell your tale,
Whale my whale.

AN OUTDATED IDEA

An outdated idea is like
An outdated style.
Nobody cares about it,
And it goes away after a while.
The idea of prejudice
Is very outdated.
Judging another's feelings, family,
Or body can make one seem jaded.

This makes the judging of race
Something more than dirt bag-like.
The amount of protein in skin
Does not decide whether they do wrong or right.
White, Black, Hispanic, Mixed, Muslim, Asian, and Indian,
Are like all other words by the human race... invented.
Many innocent men go to jail for no reason
Because of the stereotypes that society has rented.

A black boy in Texas, with a life
Much more sad and poor than yours and mine,
Was misguided, confused, and shot a man,
Then was sentenced to jail with ten years for his crime.
In the same state, a white, evil, and spoiled teen,

Had driven drunk and killed a group of four.
He is now relaxing, drinking, swimming,
And says a fake condition "affluenza" makes him deserve more.

All races in whatever parts of the world,
However, suffer in different ways.
Ever since September 11th of 2001,
The idea of all middle-easterners being dangerous is what stays.
The idea that when we need rifles to protect us from harmless people
Is more childish than a young woman like I can conceive.
It makes me beyond disappointed that this is the kind of garbage
Myself, other youths, and future generations receive.

If we can stop prejudice or not, may be an outdated idea.
Bob Dylan says, "The answer is blowing in the wind."
But we should try our hardest to help all, regardless of race,
And see if the future of our world can be peaceful again.

THE BALLAD OF HICKOCK AND SMITH

Hickock and Smith were two kindred souls.
Homosexual maybe, prostitutes don't prove anything,
But they were fake friends, and murdered four people,
Then permanently accepted the consequences it did bring.

If only Tex and Flo Smith were more responsible,
If only Hickock didn't hate his wife so much,
Then maybe they could feel love
And then gracefully love others as such.

The Clutter family was America's family,
So conventional, simple and free.
Living on a small farm house
Which was how they knew it should be.

Mr. Clutter had a sweet wife and four good kids.
"No drinking, no smoking, always pray," he said,
"Don't date no bad boys,
But if you do I'll love you anyway."

Mrs. Clutter was old and tired often,
But she was still a dear.
She was oblivious to anything out of the norm,
Including that night when she met her worst fear.

The elder sisters were not mentioned very much;
But the Clutters loved all their children the same.
The kids (and grandson) would worship Christ,
School was not a game,

Certainly not to pretty Nancy Clutter.
She had lots of friends and knew how to make a cherry pie,
Smart, over-achiever, more popular than a mean girl...
That was the title she held before she had to die.

Kenyon was the youngest, only son,
And the Daddy's boy till the day he was found dead.
"Right now he leans towards being an engineer, or a scientist,
But you can't tell me my boy's not a born rancher." Mr. Clutter said.

Nancy's boyfriend Bobby had just left,
And when he was just about to leave, he felt a little fright,
He assumed someone or thing watching him in the bushes.
Boy, he probably wished he had spent time with Nancy longer that night.

Before all this, Dick Hickock and Perry Smith
Were driving around in Kansas, talking about poetry.
Then Dick talked about his family, and Perry rambled about some parrot.
Dick told him to shut up, and contradicted with "Love ya, baby."

Their mission was so simple.

Find the safe Floyd Wells told them about,

Kill any witnesses, then vacation off in Mexico.

The men were smiling inanely, turning the next route.

Richard Eugene Hickock was a born a average boy,

Kind mother, strict father, a great athlete, a good life.

He did some petty crimes trying to be a tough, tough guy

Yet Dick was a simple car painter, with 3 kids and a wife.

Dick decided to get rich quick,

"I'm a normal" he would say. So to prove it,

He made the plan with Perry; they'd kill the family,

Steal the money, and then be on their way.

Perry Edward Smith was the sensitive one.

He had sad eyes, a sick-twisted mind, but a precious smile.

He'd wet his bed, cry in a blink, and wanted to kill himself or

Others many times. Probably from being beaten by nuns as a child.

"Something had to be wrong with us to do the

Thing we did." Perry would whisper to Dick,

But Dick would later turn on him,

Just as Perry's own father had... the prick.

So with those background stories in mind,
Our anti-heroes had arrived around midnight.
Most of the Clutters were asleep, so to kill
The awake ones, which they just might...

Dick of course played tough guy
And let Perry handle weapons and all.
A slight mistake for both of them,
Especially when the time came to face the law...

But that would wait for a while,
For now they would ask the sleepy Herb Clutter
In a broad man voice where the safe was, and if he didn't tell,
They'd slit his throat and threaten to leave him in the gutter.

He said there was no safe, which there wasn't,
But of course our criminals didn't believe him.
They shoved him around some more, threatened him again.
The fact that Clutter was telling the truth was unfathomable to them.

However, Perry Smith knew that Mr. Clutter wasn't lying,
He told his partner that they should leave after Dick scared Mrs.
Clutter too,
Dick said "No"; despite the crazy that was in Perry's eyes
That went well with the deeds he was about to do.

Mrs. Clutter was sobbing and said there was no money safe,
Dick told her to shut up, then screamed for Perry to tie her.
The "bonded" parents pleaded to the criminals not to hurt their kids,
But they just ignored them, as well as stole what was there.

Dick made Kenyon get up and go downstairs where Herb was,
He then sneered and jeered at Nancy awake and upset in her room.
Knocking on the walls like a "nutty woodpecker" Dick was,
It was chaotic that night, who's only light was the moon.

Perry was in Nancy's room.
He was looking for any loose change or hint of money.
Finding a silver dollar, he asked her about horses, about school,
"I only made it to 3rd grade!" he said trying to be funny.

Perry stopped Dick from raping Nancy,
They didn't find what they were looking for;
So they killed everyone in the house, and made off
With less than 100 dollars, wanting more.

They still vacationed in Mexico and Florida,
Bought some whores and some pancakes,
Spent time at the beach,
And argued with their lives at high stakes.

Police officer Alvin Dewey had been working long
And hard to find the sinners who killed the good small town folks.
They found the two crooks in their vacation spot, after Dick
Announced his opinions of the cops through cruel jokes.

The town was relieved, but cursed the pair of men.
Unlike Capote and Lee, they wanted them to by dead on the spot.
The officers took notice, putting Dick in the jail
And Perry in a smaller one at an older lady's house, under a tight lock.

The lawyers had tried to plead for insanity.
A reasonable verdict for one of the two,
But Midwestern folks didn't know what that meant, demanded death,
So there was no chance for you know who.

It was on the day of April 14th, 1965.
Richard E. Hickock and Perry E. Smith were executed then.
Dick first and Perry next,
Where the gallows had snickering guards, watching with their close kin.

This wasn't to make you chose a side,
To decide whose fate was better without or with,
It was a poem of Capote's excellent true novel,
It was The Ballad of Hickock and Smith.

WHITE EYES

White eyes upon blue sky,
Wet mountains on the ever dying
Earth nurses birds who come from
Long, long distances.

Ice fills empty halls
And manifests itself into the
Cracks of man's icy soul.
You fall through the depths of your own.

Forever alone the
Wolf trudging on
Frozen blue land, amoral on
The nature of law and of
Authority, you feel different.
Moses preached where you once
Stood, high on mighty power.
But you feel no rush intensifying
The black hole in your life.

REBEL KID

Daddy said don't go into town,
He still decided to go.
They heard his name,
They played his game.
The rebel boy.

He lives in his van.
It's because he can.
Because he ran
And ran.
The rebel boy.

Try to find him,
And you'll die.
If you fall in love with him,
You'll cry.
But if you meet him,
Don't defeat him,
Just smile and say "hi".

The rebel boy.

THE POETS OF EAST EDEN

The time of the rise and set of the
Sun on the east of Eden
Is where you will see
The five poets.

Led by the wisest,
They write and play
Their instruments of love
From dusk till dawn.

The wisest will lead them,
Just as how he created them.
Through every trouble and triumph,
He will keep them together.

The bravest will protect them.
Cementing them as one, contributing
Like a young soldier,
He will keep them from harm.

The inventive one will make their minds fresh.

Lovingly making something for

Their minds to feed on, to grasp.

He will keep them motivated.

The eldest will show them the way.

The way of love, right, wrong, and life.

It is surely not for the inexperienced

He shall keep them young, but intelligent.

Last, but certainly not least, The Prophet.

Hating to be called by His true calling,

He is the <u>true</u> wise man of the clan.

He is the way, the truth, and the light of the five.

With this unbelievable strength they all possess,

The beautiful creations that they all make,

And the unbelievable love they have for another,

They are the only true leaders of the world.

WILD MAN (FOR LOU REED)

As I sit in the middle of a
Lonesome hallway, my mind
Floats away to thoughts of
The Wild Man.

The Wild Man, who passed
Away just two days ago, is now
Jumping around trees and bounding
Through endless waving wheat fields.

A thought such as this is interrupted
By those who question and criticize him
And me, but you should never dislike
What you can't understand.

He may be watching you and me,
May be laughing at our petty words,
But I will love him the same as
He loves me.

BOB DYLAN DOESN'T CRY

"Nobody feels any pain."
He's right,
Not even the skeleton keys in the rain
Can know what it's like to defend your hero...
But I do.

I love the Jewish-born
Robert Allen Zimmerman
From Duluth Minnesota.
I hope he likes me.
He shouldn't though.
I'm awful.

I love you, R.A.Z
Don't let anyone pigeon-hole you.
Please don't cry in a video,
Just in front of me,
So we may weep together...

God help the poets.

Too Long a Wait, Too Short a Time

Dry leaves are lost on the trees,
Mice are even hibernating,
It is their choice it seems.
The schools are open,
But why?
This weather is unenjoyable
For everyone and you.

Snow is a no show.
Why pray for it to come when
You know it won't?
It is not in your power.

W.T.F.?

Beauty graces your evil face.

Niceness has no sign or trace.

Waxy earlobes stick to your brain

With disgusting kisses they find

Soothingly and peacefully attractive.

They don't know love... the heathens.

May your beauty shine through

Your white, supple face, have no

Shame in your fatness.

You are sneakier than a devil in your

Ways, just a fucking devil, wandering

Around your twisted little maze

As if you were Pan.

May preacher Harry Powell knife

You and yours come to think of it.

No, come to think of it, that's too harsh.

May pit bull puppies bite your nose.

Then, may you walk gracefully to a piano,

And play boogie-woogie songs, Tim Burton style.

GOVERNMENT PLAYGROUND

As I walk through a herd of
Unworthy souls, I
Understand the crossed feelings
While we're at the Government Playground.

The crossed feelings, that is,
Are the ones which an unholy
Spirit of animosity for life
Overwhelms one with unknown
Feelings of hatred, frustration,
Devastation, and disappointment.

The spirit does not conquer all,
As a matter of fact, it doesn't
Conquer many of the thousands,
But the few it does conquer
Are absolute shadows of themselves.

These ghastly feelings dragging
The victim like wild stallions
Into a brick wall, but the
Victims want this to happen.
Just another day at the Government Playground.

GHOSTLY WOMAN

White lace all over your dress

You and your many men,

They cry, they laugh, they make a mess.

It's a miracle you still love your kin.

Nobody seems nice,

But everyone cares about you.

You won't see it in their eye,

But they love you through fire and ice.

May you be young at heart,

And be wise beyond your years.

May you and your best friends never be apart,

And may joyful laughter be the only time you shed tears.

ROCK N' ROLL OPERA

"FREEDOM!"
"FREEDOM!"
"FREEDOM!"
Said mother of the so-called
Anti-Christs, also known as
Their sons.

The black snake pulls in,
The unveiling of the creator,
Through its unforgiving eyes.
It appears through the last
Eye; Demons, also known as
The band.

The group of people,
For or against them,
Are pulsating.
Screams are deafening
"Unholy!" or "FUCK YEA!"
Is heard.

As the Demons walk through

Protest and praises,

They feel no pain;

Mental or physical,

Due to Magic Leaf sickles,

Known as dope.

They hit center stage,

Crowd is insane,

The demon's headquarters,

Known as a concert, better

Known, the best fucking

Night out ever.

It Smells Like Florida

It's dark now.
Philip Seymour Hoffman died a few hours ago.
Bob Dylan is on two Super Bowl ads,
U2 might have one as well.
I still remember Pete Seeger.

I don't know what Florida smells like exactly,
I imagine pot, gas, smoke,
No palm trees or ocean,
But I did taste salt.

I know the States don't have a fragrance,
Unless you include the smell of "Freedom"...
Sighs.
You know though,
The two times I've been to Florida,
I really enjoyed those smells. No sarcasm.

(Probably because nobody told me Florida had those smells...)

CHUNK

Wet drunk dead

Alive well drunk

One lives, the other dies

BUILDING YOUR NAME

Burroughs is right about nearly anything.
If he could, he would agree,
But I wonder what he'd say exactly.

I myself wonder why it takes me so long to finish
Long poems. My publisher would scream at me if
He knew what I was originally going to write.

I hope school goes well...
It should be a fascinating day at pre-school penitentiary.
In the mean time I'll slowly build a name for myself.

MY POET DOES IT GOOD

Who are you really, my love?
Why do you hide in the bushes of Woodstock,
Never edging toward your true calling,
And not feeling an urge to rock?

It's me I want you to love,
Not that ugly witch you call "Pretty".
You may also love the girl with the Egyptian ring,
The gospel beauties, or the teenage girl in the city.

Please listen to your friends,
And to the people that REALLY love you.
I don't mean to be a brown-noser,
But I'm inspired by your lyrics and words too.

THE QUARTET PRACTICED IN THE PARK

Yellow, Blue, Orange, Pink,

But with colors inside one another.

Deaths to all Pigs...

Who copy you.

May you have love forever and be loved forever,

For better or for worse that is.

I won't make you sing, just love you.

All YOU need is love.

WATER TRUNK TEAR

Old Man Powell pulls up Mary's sweater
To try and see if he could know her better,
But Mary isn't Mary.
Mary, is actually, quite, hairy.

P. Ness, the poet, lives on Mars,
Picks up boys, and is married to his sister, P. Lars.
All the while, he has beautiful feet.
So nice, V. Gyna came to his Cub Scout meet.

Mr. Universe asked Lou C. Fur
To send his son-in-law some Myrrh.
Fur responded, "The one amazon.com has got?
They'll send it on a robot!"

FOR DRANEY

Lonely as the Jesus of old,
You have been lied to.
Your face has been through pain
For the pure pleasure of others.

If men were born alone,
Then no one would have lived.
However by the cruelness of mankind
Everyone would wish to die

Only fools wouldn't agree to this.
The working man would simply shrug it off.
Although the pain is obvious,
None will care when it's too late.

Though love is challenged by hate,
And vice versa,
Love is the old fashioned emotion.
Old-fashioned isn't popular.

The last rites of the world
Will be on a sticky note,
Then tossed into a rain puddle,
Never to be read again.

FOR PETE SEEGER

Nobody knows the physique of the artist.
Knowing is not seeing with our eyes.
Vision is not seeing with our heart.
We are all speaking through truths lies.

The morning symbols from the breeze of the day came through the rocky,
Vacant mountains of my mind.
The last time anyone walked through the mind had been the last
Destination of their journey though being with the poetic kind.

Your words may touch the thousands that read it,
Or just the one elderly soul still behind his time.
The minute you spend reading this will be the minute
You can be trying to write your own rhythm and rhyme.

Break time can wait a half hour,
TV can wait too,
Try to read and reread some work of yours,
Because the best art ever made was you.

DIRTY MAN

Dirty man
Sitting on the wet bench,
With a cold ass
And no friends.

The watching policeman wonders by,
And arrests him for drug possession,
Although all he had,
Was an empty bottle of medication for schizophrenia.

At night it rains.
It thunders and pours
While the dirty man covers himself
With newspaper and leaves.

His cup is filled at midnight
Up to the brim.
It's practically overflowing with
Rain and tears.

He waves at passersby.

With his cardboard sign in hand,

Women scoff, mothers pull their children away,

Frat boys spit and throw items, sorority girls giggle.

As the quick day ends,

A stray puppy licks the exposed toes from sock.

He laughs, a rare action for him, and strokes it's back.

He is then killed in a drive by shooting.

TRY AND GET

If you try and get,
You won't get what you try.
But trying isn't getting,
Especially when you try.
You try and try and try
But you won't get.

THESE TEARS ARE FROM EARLIER

Tomorrow is Valentine's Day,
But these tears are from earlier,
From when I wanted you to stay
In my heart,
In my art,
You would have left anyways

The tears I cry aren't from sorrow,
But from pity,
On how he left you and had to go,
You were tough for what you did,
You're a big girl, kid.
He was confused during his show.

So I say "Don't get girly-er."
I'll see you soon,
Hopefully me and he,
We have time together before we see thee,
I shed love, in these tears of earlier.

WHITE CLIFFS AND SNOW MOUNTAINS

Cat prints,
Blue stream of conscious writing,
Unloved swans,
Frozen lakes,
Inside me.

Freedom of Speech is for losers,
Rebellion and blood for winners,
Veins pop,
Children die,
Women shit in urinals
Because they can't shit themselves like men can.
Wet faces cry.

I stand
I stand on Mountains and Cliffs
On steep peaks and high rises,
Both end in big let downs,
But I'll stand here

I stand on the white cliff for hate,
Just how whites will hate
Hate long and hard

But it will end hard,

Fall hard.

Hard.

Stand on the mountains for love.

The snow melts and falls.

Melts and falls.

Love will melt and fall,

Love will be a mountain,

Rise and fall.

Rise and Fall.

RISE AND FALL.

MELT AND RISE.

MELT AND FALL.

FALL AND MELT.

FALL AND MELT.

FALL AND RISE.

FALL AND RISE.

FALL AND RISE!

I SHALL FALL AND RISE!!!...

I stand on White Cliffs and Snow Mountains.

SOME TIME LATER

Rock n' Roll is dead.
Only guitars remain.
Brought back from the dead,
Rock has risen again.
Even though it's thriving,
Time has made it a bit sick.

Alienated.
Leisurely waiting for your arrival.
Listening to see if your name is sounded,
Ester Dran, Carl Dran, Steve Drane.
None of them are names I'm looking for.

Z and on up I don't hear you.
I wait alongside a wall.
My security next to me.
My phone in my hand.
Even though I "forgot" you long ago,
Reason didn't process, still hasn't.
My only wish is you'd be alive,
And then nothing else would matter.
None of your moods would sway me.

Just as I suspected,

Only the fittest survive.

Having just the knowledge,

Nope, sorry dear.

Waiting was wasted.

In my mind shot and killed.

Neither I, nor you, would disagree.

Smiles erase from my mind.

Taking away all other memories.

Only your note remains,

No hot-tempered Lufkin whore can take it away.

Leaving and getting on the bike,

Either spouseless or un-spouseless,

Not one impulse is the same as when I first came.

Narrating this seems silly.

Of all the people he knew,

No one else showed up but me...

Great things have happened to me.

Riding out of the gate, I look back,

At all of the stuff that I accomplished.

Having met all my idols,

And being one of the world's newest writers...
My thought then switches to you.

Around when we were together,
Right was wrong and vice-versa.
Though I never did anything "bad",
Heroes were forgotten at the time,
Unless they were a Heavy Metal band.
Remember our <u>insightful</u> conversations?

Choosing the path that you choose,
Having the knowledge you had,
And doing the stuff you did,
Prison was more than likely.
Maybe we could've stayed together...
Another life time, perhaps.
No chance it'll happen even then.

Caring about you is insane,
Having it be my natural impulse coming here is worse.
Another crazy part was your influence,
Riding a motorcycle, ME?
Letting go is like spitting in the wind,
Either way you get it out, it comes back,
Splatting upside your temple forever.

Letting go of you should be easy-

Unless you were particularly attractive.

Try not to think about that-

Wait, that's vain on both sides.

It is in my opinion only, by the way.

Do NOT think I hate you either,

Graciously, I adore you,

Even if you don't feel the same.

Driving in the, well, parking in the driveway,

Only one memory remains-

Do you remember 8th grade?

Going around the locker bays,

Even commenting each other

Saying, "Nice shirt!"

Only we could say that to each other.

No one else is Rock n' Roll; just us.

I SIT ALONE, BUT NOT LONELY

O' mighty winds which rush the pale faces of the alien race;
They know not by what see, thee in close approximation,
But what will influence their souls and children's souls.
My own soul sees thee in small boxes,
Little dogs picking up and playing with
Eyeballs, fresh out of their sockets.
The dogs chew and enjoy tug of war with the tails
Of the eyeballs, and lap up the lovely popped cornea.
Faces remain inside the box, frightened;
But are eased with small licks from Chihuahuas.

The shy boys in the corner don't know what to think.
A few prostitutes and politicians share their thoughts,
"Well how did you find the young one?"
"I think he was unknowingly terrified if the unknown.",
And so on and so forth.
The doctor in the upper hall gives a long laugh.
He passes out and a old woman resuscitates him
Then he punches her in the face.
There were no survivors.
The best is either coming or present,
Many don't know where to look.
My own motivation was not present on that day.

I love all of the great thinkers,
Motivators, Peace makers, lovers,
Kissers, Rockers, Knockers,
Rebels, Civils, and Bastards.
I love Bob Dylan, Maya Angelou, John Lennon,
Allen Ginsberg, Lewis Carroll, and Patti Smith.
I am a hypocrite of poets.

MUSTARD PANCAKES
(THE POEM NOT THE SHOW)

"Bound under 2 rivers"...
No, it's not the same.
Too many people use that line
In poems.

Maybe not enough,
I dunno.
I don't read poems.